The Book of the Home

Celebrate your home's story

bluemoonbell

www.bluemoonbell.com

Illustrations by Dave Ruffner
ISBN: 978-0692185797

A Special Invitation

Welcome to the premium home-focused experience of Blue Moon Bell. Our mission is to help you foster a home refuge from which you may dream and de-stress.

In appreciation of your support, we would like to offer you our

FREE GUIDE,

which will help you get started building a home retreat. We know what you're thinking . . . There is no such thing as free! What's the catch? Well, this is the one time where something isn't too good to be true. There's nothing to buy, no credit card to give, or some other "gotcha." Simply provide your e-mail address, or message us, and we'll send you our FREE GUIDE containing expert tips for de-stressing and building your home retreat.

This special offer is reserved for our Book of the Home customers. To claim your guide, simply visit the website below:

www.bluemoonbell.com/pages/guide

---

*This book belongs to the above named home and
should remain with its owners.*

This book was first presented to this home on

_____

By

_____

"The house shelters day-dreaming, the house protects the dreamer, the house allows one to dream in peace."

~ Gaston Bachelard, *French philosopher*

Table of Contents

Introduction

This book should remain with the home and serve as a living history of the structure, its residents, and its evolution over time. The details you note within these pages will help you remember all those events and occurrences that are otherwise so forgettable, and for those that follow you will provide an invaluable history of your house and its community.

Whether you are the first resident of a new structure or the latest dweller in a historic home, try and make every effort to document your own memories and uncover previously unrecorded details.

Depending on the age of the property, considerable research may be required to bring to light as much as possible of the past. A helpful starting point for your research might be the previous deeds of the home, which are usually on file at the county recorder's office, along with the property's permits, inspections, appraisals, and tax assessments. Other beneficial paperwork includes the chain of title, held by the county courthouse, and the tax records. Of course, the institutional knowledge of your neighborhood, its residents, and local business owners can prove invaluable.

When you come to fill in those details which only past residents will know, then it is only by finding these people and meeting or corresponding with them that any details will emerge. This may prove to be a fascinating research.

Following your study of the objective aspects of your home, we encourage you to record your Moments of Joy in the home. Kindly frame these memories to inspire the future occupants and thereby cultivate a chain of similar, future feelings towards your home.

The Book of the Home is your home's keepsake, which is yours only temporarily. From that perspective, it is a *Book of Dreams*, as it offers a platform to speak to future home-dwellers. This book will give you much pleasure and contentment in your home. May it help you foster your own home refuge—space and time to dream and aspire!

The Home

The Construction

The creation of a new house is an exciting time, when a parcel of land is shaped into a beloved home.
Use the space below to describe your land, prior to development, and the details
of your home's initial construction.

Land Use, prior to construction:

Date of Groundbreaking:

Date of Completion:

Seller:

Buyer:

Cost of Land:

Cost of Construction:

Developers:

Architects:

Builders:

Additional Notes:

Buying & Selling

A well-built house will shelter many families throughout its lifetime.
Please note the details of your purchase to create a complete record of all homeowners.

Property Transactions	1st	2nd	3rd
Date of Sale:			
Seller:			
Real Estate Agent:			
Attorney:			
Buyer:			
Real Estate Agent:			
Attorney:			
Asking Price:			
Purchase Price:			
Additional Details:			

The Home

4th	5th	6th	7th

Exterior Details

Your first impression of your home began with its exterior details. Use the following pages to describe the structure's outward appearance and any changes you have made over the years.

If information on the original state of the house exists, note those details below; otherwise, explain the home as it was at your purchase.

Home Structure

Original State:

Architectural Style:

Exterior Building Materials:

Roofing Material:

Chimney Style:

Door Color/Type:

Home Structure, con't

Original State:

Window Trim/Shutters:

Deck/Porch Description:

Additional Features:

Alterations

Date	Type of Alteration	Designer/Architect	Cost/Details

Garden & Grounds

Attach Original Plot Plan

Original State:

Lawn Cover:

Distinctive Bushes and Flowers:

Trees (Species and Placement):

Lighting Features:

Garage/Shed:

Driveway:

Additional Features (i.e., Boundaries):

Alterations

Date	Type of Alteration	Designer/Architect	Cost/Details

The Neighborhood

Original state of the neighborhood:

Street:

Street Lighting:

Adjacent Properties:

Accessible Public Transportation:

Nearby Shops and Restaurants:

School District:

Additional Neighborhood Features:

Changes

Date	Type of Change	Additional Details

Interior Details

The true spirit of a home lies within its walls. Use the following pages to describe your home's layout, interior design, utilities, and more.

If information on the original state of the house exists, note those details below; otherwise, explain the home as it was at your purchase.

Floor Plans:

Please sketch each original floor plan and label rooms with numbers to correspond with the subsequent room descriptions. Add as much detail as possible, and depict structural additions/changes in a contrasting color.

Basement   First Floor   Second Floor

Third Floor   Fourth Floor   Attic/Fifth Floor

Interior Details

Major Alterations

Date	Type of Alteration	Designer/Architect	Cost/Details

Room Descriptions

Basement

Dimensions:

Ceiling Height:

Interior Design Details:

Walls:

Ceiling:

Floor:

Doors/Doorways:

Windows:

Light Fixtures:

Trim:

Other:

General Description of Room and Function (interior design changes over time, etc.)

Room 1

Dimensions:

Ceiling Height:

Interior Design Details:

    Walls:

    Ceiling:

    Floor:

    Doors/Doorways:

    Windows:

    Light Fixtures:

    Trim:

Other:

General Description of Room and Function (interior design changes over time, etc.)

Room 2

Dimensions:

Ceiling Height:

Interior Design Details:

Walls:

Ceiling:

Floor:

Doors/Doorways:

Windows:

Light Fixtures:

Trim:

Other:

General Description of Room and Function (interior design changes over time, etc.)

Room 3

Dimensions:

Ceiling Height:

Interior Design Details:

Walls:

Ceiling:

Floor:

Doors/Doorways:

Windows:

Light Fixtures:

Trim:

Other:

General Description of Room and Function (interior design changes over time, etc.)

Room 4

Dimensions:

Ceiling Height:

Interior Design Details:

    Walls:

    Ceiling:

    Floor:

    Doors/Doorways:

    Windows:

    Light Fixtures:

    Trim:

Other:

General Description of Room and Function (interior design changes over time, etc.)

Room 5

Dimensions:

Ceiling Height:

Interior Design Details:

Walls:

Ceiling:

Floor:

Doors/Doorways:

Windows:

Light Fixtures:

Trim:

Other:

General Description of Room and Function (interior design changes over time, etc.)

Room 6

Dimensions:

Ceiling Height:

Interior Design Details:

Walls:

Ceiling:

Floor:

Doors/Doorways:

Windows:

Light Fixtures:

Trim:

Other:

General Description of Room and Function (interior design changes over time, etc.)

Room 7

Dimensions:

Ceiling Height:

Interior Design Details:

    Walls:

    Ceiling:

    Floor:

    Doors/Doorways:

    Windows:

    Light Fixtures:

    Trim:

Other:

General Description of Room and Function (interior design changes over time, etc.)

Room 8

Dimensions:

Ceiling Height:

Interior Design Details:

Walls:

Ceiling:

Floor:

Doors/Doorways:

Windows:

Light Fixtures:

Trim:

Other:

General Description of Room and Function (interior design changes over time, etc.)

Room 9

Dimensions:

Ceiling Height:

Interior Design Details:

    Walls:

    Ceiling:

    Floor:

    Doors/Doorways:

    Windows:

    Light Fixtures:

    Trim:

Other:

General Description of Room and Function (interior design changes over time, etc.)

Room 10

Dimensions:

Ceiling Height:

Interior Design Details:

    Walls:

    Ceiling:

    Floor:

    Doors/Doorways:

    Windows:

    Light Fixtures:

    Trim:

Other:

General Description of Room and Function (interior design changes over time, etc.)

Room 11

Dimensions:

Ceiling Height:

Interior Design Details:

   Walls:

   Ceiling:

   Floor:

   Doors/Doorways:

   Windows:

   Light Fixtures:

   Trim:

Other:

General Description of Room and Function (interior design changes over time, etc.)

Room 12

Dimensions:

Ceiling Height:

Interior Design Details:

    Walls:

    Ceiling:

    Floor:

    Doors/Doorways:

    Windows:

    Light Fixtures:

    Trim:

Other:

General Description of Room and Function (interior design changes over time, etc.)

Room 13

Dimensions:

Ceiling Height:

Interior Design Details:

    Walls:

    Ceiling:

    Floor:

    Doors/Doorways:

    Windows:

    Light Fixtures:

    Trim:

Other:

General Description of Room and Function (interior design changes over time, etc.)

Room 14

Dimensions:

Ceiling Height:

Interior Design Details:

　　Walls:

　　Ceiling:

　　Floor:

　　Doors/Doorways:

　　Windows:

　　Light Fixtures:

　　Trim:

Other:

General Description of Room and Function (interior design changes over time, etc.)

Room 15

Dimensions:

Ceiling Height:

Interior Design Details:

Walls:

Ceiling:

Floor:

Doors/Doorways:

Windows:

Light Fixtures:

Trim:

Other:

General Description of Room and Function (interior design changes over time, etc.)

Room 16

Dimensions:

Ceiling Height:

Interior Design Details:

Walls:

Ceiling:

Floor:

Doors/Doorways:

Windows:

Light Fixtures:

Trim:

Other:

General Description of Room and Function (interior design changes over time, etc.)

Room 17

Dimensions:

Ceiling Height:

Interior Design Details:

Walls:

Ceiling:

Floor:

Doors/Doorways:

Windows:

Light Fixtures:

Trim:

Other:

General Description of Room and Function (interior design changes over time, etc.)

Room 18

Dimensions:

Ceiling Height:

Interior Design Details:

Walls:

Ceiling:

Floor:

Doors/Doorways:

Windows:

Light Fixtures:

Trim:

Other:

General Description of Room and Function (interior design changes over time, etc.)

Attic

Dimensions:

Ceiling Height:

Interior Design Details:

   Walls:

   Ceiling:

   Floor:

   Doors/Doorways:

   Windows:

   Light Fixtures:

   Trim:

Other:

General Description of Room and Function (interior design changes over time, etc.)

Utilities

	Original Details/Description	Alterations or Changes
Air Conditioning:		
Heat:		
Gas:		
Electric:		
Water:		
Cable:		
Internet (e.g., SSIDs):		
Telephone:		

	Original Details/Description	*Alterations or Changes*
Sewage:		
Security System:		
Garbage Removal:		
Recycling/Composting:		
Other:		

Additional Notes:

The Home Dwellers

The Families

A home is so much more than bricks, pipes, and floor plans.

In this section, describe the residents of your home, who bring the life and warmth into its rooms.

Surname	Dates of Residency

The Family Members

Surname:

Name	Age	Occupation	Arrival	Departure

Pets:

Name	Species	Description	Arrival	Departure

Additional Details:

The Family Members

Surname:

Name	Age	Occupation	Arrival	Departure

Pets:

Name	Species	Description	Arrival	Departure

Additional Details:

The Family Members

Surname:

Name	Age	Occupation	Arrival	Departure

Pets:

Name	Species	Description	Arrival	Departure

Additional Details:

The Family Members

Surname:

Name	Age	Occupation	Arrival	Departure

Pets:

Name	Species	Description	Arrival	Departure

Additional Details:

The Family Members

Surname:

Name	Age	Occupation	Arrival	Departure

Pets:

Name	Species	Description	Arrival	Departure

Additional Details:

The Family Members

Surname:

Name	Age	Occupation	Arrival	Departure

Pets:

Name	Species	Description	Arrival	Departure

Additional Details:

The Family Members

Surname:

Name	Age	Occupation	Arrival	Departure

Pets:

Name	Species	Description	Arrival	Departure

Additional Details:

The Family Members

Surname:

Name	Age	Occupation	Arrival	Departure

Pets:

Name	Species	Description	Arrival	Departure

Additional Details:

The Family Members

Surname:

Name	Age	Occupation	Arrival	Departure

Pets:

Name	Species	Description	Arrival	Departure

Additional Details:

The Family Members

Surname:

Name	Age	Occupation	Arrival	Departure

Pets:

Name	Species	Description	Arrival	Departure

Additional Details:

The Family Members

Surname:

Name	Age	Occupation	Arrival	Departure

Pets:

Name	Species	Description	Arrival	Departure

Additional Details:

The Home Records

The Owners

Surname(s)	Dates of Ownership

Home Receipts & Expenses

Fixed Assets (kitchen built-ins, heating and air-conditioning, roofing, etc.)

Date	Description	Price

Utility Expenses (electric, gas, sewage, water, telephone, cable etc.)

Date	Description	Price

Maintenance Expenses

Date	Description	Price

Additional Expenses

Date	Description	Price

Photographs

Please use these pages to affix photographs of the home's exterior, interior, and residents.

Photographs

Original Plot Plans

Please list original plot plans for your home and landscaping.

	Date	Description
1)		
2)		
3)		
4)		
5)		
6)		
7)		
8)		
9)		

Construction Plans & Blueprints

Please document plans and blueprints for structural changes made to your house.

	Date	Description
1)		
2)		
3)		
4)		
5)		
6)		
7)		
8)		
9)		

Moments of Joy
in the Home

Moments of Joy in the Home

Kindly describe moments of joy, which may inspire future occupants and cultivate an ongoing chain of similar feelings towards your home.